Olivia

By Dina Maiben

Editorial Committee:

Sarah Gluck
Lesley Litman
Ellen J. Rank

For Carmela S. Nielsen, my first Hebrew teacher,
from whom I learned the Alef Bet.

"If I have seen further it is by standing on the shoulders of giants."
—Isaac Newton

Dina Maiben

Book and cover design: Hazan + Co.
Illustration: Curt Walstead
Project editor: Terry S. Kaye

Copyright © 2012 Behrman House, Inc.
Springfield, New Jersey
www.behrmanhouse.com

ISBN 978-0-87441-860-6

Behrman House, Inc.
www.behrmanhouse.com

Contents

Alef Bet Chart

Color in each letter after you learn it in *Ready, Set...Go Alef Bet!*

טַלִּית   תּוֹרָה

| Tet | ט | Tav | תּ ת | **WHAT'S NEW?** |

Off to the "Right" Start

Look at the Hebrew words below. Your teacher will read them to you.
Circle every letter with a "t" sound.

3. תַּלְמוּד   2. טוֹב   1. תּוֹרָה

6. טֶלֶוִיזְיָה   5. תְּפִילָה   4. טֶלֶפוֹן

Draw an arrow pointing to the first letter of each word above.
On what side do Hebrew words start?

Hebrew words start on the _____ side.

5

Color the ת.

The new letter ת or ת
looks like it has a **T**oe.

Color the ט.

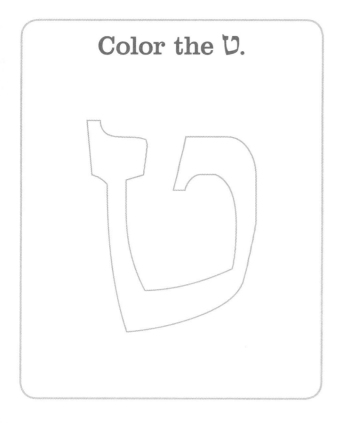

The new letter ט is open
on **T**op.

I Can Understand Hebrew!

Your teacher will read this word to you:

עַל

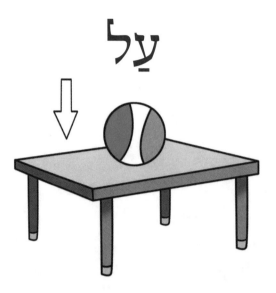

Your teacher will read this sentence to you.
Circle the picture that matches the sentence.

טַלִית עַל תּוֹרָה.

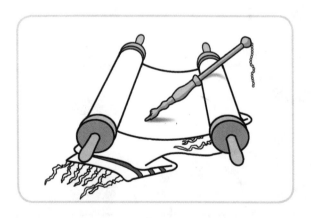

Now I Know My Alef-Bet!

Complete the **T**av. Then write two of each kind on your own.

Complete the **T**et. Then write three on your own.

Sound Check

The names of these objects sound similar in Hebrew and English.
Circle all the objects that begin with the letters ט and ת.

Game On

How many objects did you circle? _____
Use this number to score bonus points in the Jungle Jump game in *Ready Set...Go Alef Bet!* online.

שָׁלוֹם

שַׁבָּת

Shin שׁ WHAT'S NEW?

Color the שׁ.

Letter Hint
The new letter שׁ looks like a **SH**ip.

Now I Know My Alef-Bet!

Complete the **Sh**in. Then write three on your own.

Letter by Letter

Circle the Hebrew letter that begins each word. You may circle the same letter more than once in a row.

שׁ	תּ	שׁ	ט	
תּ	שׁ	שׁ	תּ	
ט	שׁ	שׁ	ט	
תּ	שׁ	תּ	ט	

I Can Understand Hebrew!

Your teacher will read this phrase to you:

שַׁבָּת שָׁלוֹם!

Check all the pictures that match the greeting above.

Sound Check

Circle all the objects that begin with the sound of שׁ.

Hint: If you have not yet learned the Hebrew name of an item, it has a similar name in Hebrew and English.

Game On

Write the first letter of the words you circled. _____
Use this answer to score bonus points in the Hip Hop Hebrew game in
Ready Set…Go Alef Bet! online.

YAHOO! 3

יָד

Yud   ל

Take a Closer Look!

On each line cross out any letter that is different from the one in the box.

שׁ	ט	שׁ	שׁ	שׁ .1
ל	ל	שׁ	ל	ל .2
ט	שׁ	ט	ל	ט .3

Color the ׳

so it looks like **Y**our hand.

Letter Hint

The new letter ׳ looks like **Y**our hand.

Now I Know My Alef-Bet!

Complete the **Y**ud. Then write three on your own.

ך ך֡ ך

Did You Know?

When we read from the Torah we do not touch the words with our hands. Instead, we use a special pointer, also called a יָד, to follow the words.

I Can Understand Hebrew!

Your teacher will read this word to you:

שֻׁלְחָן

Your teacher will read these sentences to you.
Draw a line from each sentence to its matching picture.

1. תּוֹרָה עַל שֻׁלְחָן.

2. טַלִּית עַל תּוֹרָה.

3. יָד עַל תּוֹרָה.

4. יָד עַל שֻׁלְחָן.

5. טַלִּית עַל שֻׁלְחָן.

Sound Check

The names of these objects sound similar in Hebrew and English.
Cross out all the objects that do <u>not</u> begin with the sound of י.

Game On

How many objects are not crossed out? _____
Use this number to score bonus points in the Zero Gravity game in
Ready Set…Go Alef Bet! online.

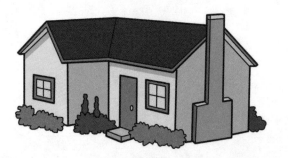

בַּיִת

Bet	בְּ	**WHAT'S NEW?**

Color the בְּ.

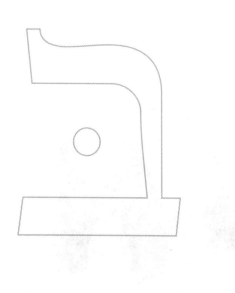

Letter Hint

The new letter בּ looks like it has a **B**elly **B**utton.

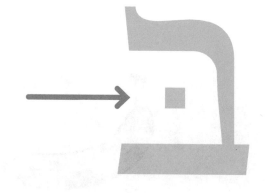

Now I Know My Alef-Bet!

Complete the **B**et. Then write three on your own.

Sound Check

The names of these objects sound similar in Hebrew and English.
Circle all the objects that begin with the sound of בּ.

I Can Understand Hebrew!

Your teacher will read this word part to you:

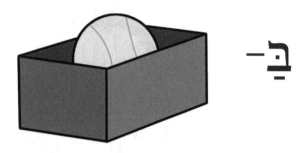

בְּ–

Your teacher will read these sentences to you. In each picture cross out the object that is not in the sentence.

2. טַלִּית עַל שֻׁלְחָן.

1. שֻׁלְחָן בַּבַּיִת.

4. יָד עַל תּוֹרָה.

3. יָד בַּיָּד.

"Open Your Mouth and Say 'Ah'!"

Hebrew vowels are dots and dashes. They are written under, over, or after letters.

"Ah" = ☐ ☐ ☐

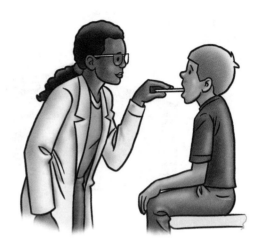

 Word Building

Read each line aloud.

START

תַּ   טָ   תַ   טַ   תָּ   .1

שַׁ   שַׁ   שָׁ   שָׁ   שַׁ   .2

יַ   יַ   יָ   יַ   יָ   .3

בַ   בָּ   בָּ   בַ   בַ   .4

Hidden Picture

Color in the hidden picture to find the Jewish people's most valuable possession.

Blue = "T"

Red = "Y"

Yellow = "B"

Brown = "SH"

Game On

Circle the Hebrew letter that begins the word for the picture above.

י ב ת שׁ

Use this letter to score bonus points in the Wacky Wheelbarrow game in *Ready Set…Go Alef Bet!* online.

עִפָּרוֹן | אִמָּא | אַבָּא

| Ayin | ע | Alef | א | WHAT'S NEW? |

Take a Closer Look!

On each line cross out the letter that is different from the one in the box.

י	י	ע	י	י .1
א	ת	ת	ת	ת .2
ע	ט	ע	ע	ע .3
ת	א	א	א	א .4

Letter Hint

The letters א and ע do not make sounds of their own. When an א or an ע has a vowel with it, it only makes the sound of the vowel. *Remember:* Hebrew vowels are dots and dashes under, above, or after a letter.

Color the א in blue.
Color the vowel in red.

Color the ע in green.
Color the vowel in orange.

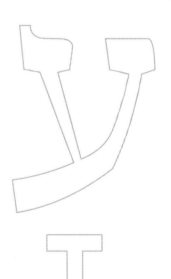

Now I Know My Alef-Bet!

Complete the **A**lef. Then write three on your own.

Complete the **A**yin. Then write three on your own.

You're an Artist!

Your teacher will read these
sentences to you. Draw a picture
to illustrate lines 1–3.

1. שַׁבָּת בַּבַּיִת.

2. אַבָּא בַּבַּיִת.

3. אִמָּא בַּבַּיִת.

4. ״שַׁבָּת שָׁלוֹם, אַבָּא.״

5. ״שַׁבָּת שָׁלוֹם, אִמָּא.״

6. שָׁלוֹם בַּבַּיִת.

Crack the Code

I'm a very special day,
For rest, for study, and for play.
Crack the code in this little game
And you will find my Hebrew name!

On each line, circle the letter that sounds the same as the one in the box.

שׁ	בּ	ת	ט	שׁ	.1
ט	בּ	שׁ	י	י	.2
שׁ	בּ	ת	ת	בּ	.3
י	שׁ	ט	בּ	ת	.4
ת	שׁ	י	בּ	ט	.5

Write the circled letters from lines 1, 3, and 5 in the numbered spaces below.

———————   ——————   ——————
    5   3   1

Game On

Use the word you filled in above to score bonus points in the Jungle Jump game in *Ready Set…Go Alef Bet!* online.

25

 שָׁלוֹם

 מְזוּזָה

Final Mem   Mem   WHAT'S NEW?

Color the מ.

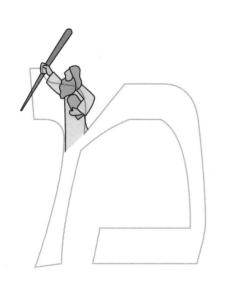

Letter Hint

The new letter מ looks like Moses on a Mountain.

 # Word Building

Read these Hebrew syllables out loud.

START

עָ	אָ	עַ	מָ	מָ	.1
שָׁ	שׁ	שָׁ	תַ	תָ	.2
מָ	מַ	מַ	בָ	בַ	.3

Color the מ

so it looks like a **M**arshmallow floating in hot cocoa. Then color the cocoa brown or tan.

Letter Hint

The new letter מ looks like a **M**arshmallow.

Now I Know My Alef-Bet!

Complete the **M**em. Then write three on your own.

Complete the Final **M**em. Then write three on your own.

Climb the Mountain!

Match each mountain to its climber.
Connect the Hebrew letters that make the same sounds.

I Can Understand Hebrew!

Your teacher will read these words to you. Match each word to its picture.

יָד .1

בַּיִת .2

שַׁבָּת .3

טַלִית .4

תּוֹרָה .5

שָׁלוֹם .6

מְזוּזָה .7

עִפָּרוֹן .8

אִמָּא .9

אַבָּא .10

Letter by Letter

Circle the Hebrew letter that begins each word.

Game On

Which letter did you circle three times? Draw a box around it below.

מ ט א

Use this letter to score bonus points in the Hip Hop Hebrew game in *Ready Set…Go Alef Bet!* online.

גְּלִידָה

Gimel   ג   WHAT'S NEW?

Color the ג.

Letter Hint

The new letter ג looks like it is Going for a walk.

Now I Know My Alef-Bet!

Complete the **G**imel. Then write three on your own.

Sound Check

The names of these objects sound similar in Hebrew and English. Cross out all the objects that do not begin with the new letter ג.

Word Building

Some syllables end in a vowel. Others end in a consonant. When a Hebrew syllable ends in a consonant, the consonant is the last sound you say.

Read these Hebrew syllables out loud.

START

עַם	אָ	בָּם	בַּ	בָּ	.1
שָׁם	שַׁ	גָם	גָ	גַ	.2
יָם	יָ	תָם	תָ	טַ	.3
יָם	תָם	עַם	גַם	בָּם	.4
תַּת	אַט	בַּת	גַת	מַט	.5

Take a Closer Look!

Circle the Hebrew letter that begins each word.

ע ט מ	ע ט מ	ע ט מ

I Can Understand Hebrew!

Your teacher will read this word to you:

גֶּשֶׁם

Your teacher will read these sentences to you.
Circle the picture that each sentence describes.

2. שֻׁלְחָן בַּגֶּשֶׁם.

1. מְזוּזָה בַּיָּד.

4. בַּיִת בַּגֶּשֶׁם.

3. עִפָּרוֹן בַּיָּד.

End Game

Say the Hebrew name of each picture out loud.
Listen for the sound at the end of the word.
Circle all the items that end with the sound of "M."

Hint: You can look back at the words on pages 9, 22, and 34. All the other words are similar in Hebrew and English.

Game On

How many objects did you circle? _____

Draw a shape around the Hebrew letter that ends the words you circled.

 שׁ   ם   ת

Use this letter to score bonus points in the Zero Gravity game in *Ready Set… Go Alef Bet!* online.

DING, DONG! 8

דֶּגֶל

Dalet   ד   WHAT'S NEW?

Color the ד.

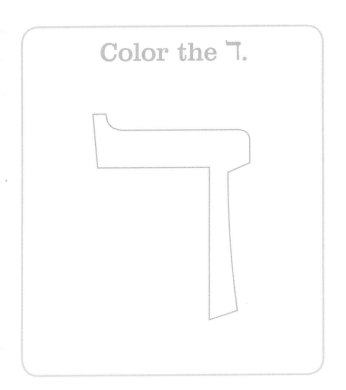

Letter Hint

The new letter ד looks like it is a **D**oor swinging open on its hinge.

36

Now I Know My Alef-Bet!

Complete the **D**alet. Then write three on your own.

In the Beginning

Circle the Hebrew letter that begins each word.

ד ג ט

ד ג ט

א ב ת

י ד מ

שׁ ע ט

ד ג ט

"Whoo-Whoo!"

 וֹ אָ

"OO" = וֹ ◻ּ

Word Building

Read each line aloud. *Remember*: When a syllable ends with a consonant, the consonant is the last sound you say.

START ►

גָ	מָ	בַּ	עֶ	דַ	1.
גְ	מְ	בּוּ	אוּ	דוּ	2.
מוּ	עֶ	גְ	דְ	יוּ	3.
מֵם	יָם	גַם	עַם	דָם	4.
מוּם יוֹם		גְ	אָ	דְ	5.

38

I Can Understand Hebrew!

Your teacher will read these words to you:

מַיִם

דָג

 ## You're an Artist!

Your teacher will read these sentences to you. Draw in what is missing from each picture.

‫1. בַּיִת בַּגֶשֶׁם.‬

‫2. דָג בַּמַיִם.‬

‫3. דוֹלְפִין בַּמַיִם.‬

‫4. אַבָּא בַּגֶשֶׁם. אִמָּא בַּגֶשֶׁם.‬

End Game

Say the Hebrew name of each picture out loud. Listen for the sound at the end of the word. Then circle the Hebrew letter that ends the word.

Hint: You can look back to the Key Words on pages 5, 9, 13, and 17.

י ד ת ם

שׁ ב ת ד

ג ע ד ת

ת ב י ג

Game On

Write the letter that was circled only once in the activity above.

_____

Use this letter to score bonus points in the Wacky Wheelbarrow game in *Ready Set…Go Alef Bet!* online.

KEEP COOL! 9

בּוֹרֵא פְּרִי הַגָּפֶן

קִדּוּשׁ

כִּפָּה

| Koof | ק | Kaf | כ | **WHAT'S NEW?** |

Color the כ.

Make the **C**ough drop any color you want.

Letter Hint

The new letter כ looks like someone with a **C**ough drop in his mouth.

Color the ק.

Now I Know My Alef-Bet!

Complete the **K**af. Then write three on your own.

Complete the **K**oof. Then write three on your own.

I Can Understand Hebrew!

Your teacher will read these words to you:

כִּתָּה

מוֹרָה

Your teacher will read these sentences to you.
Check ✔ every sentence that describes the picture.

1. _____ מוֹרָה בַּכִּתָּה.

2. _____ גְּלִידָה בַּיָד.

3. _____ אַבָּא בַּכִּתָּה.

4. _____ עִפָּרוֹן בַּיָד.

5. _____ בַּיִת בַּגֶּשֶׁם.

6. _____ דָּג בַּכִּתָּה.

7. _____ עִפָּרוֹן עַל שֻׁלְחָן.

8. _____ דָּג עַל שֻׁלְחָן.

43

Crack the Code

On each line, circle the letter that does not make the sound in the box on the right.

כ	כ	ק	בּ	ק	כ	כ	**K** .1
עֶ	י	עָ	אֶ	עַ	אָ	עֶ	**AH** .2
ד	ד	ד	ד	ד	ת	ד	**D** .3
בּ	בּ	בּ	ג	בּ	בּ	בּ	**B** .4
מ	ס	שׁ	מ	ם	מ	מ	**M** .5
ט	ת	ט	ת	תּ	ם	ט	**T** .6

Write the circled letters in the numbered spaces below.

___	___	___	___	___	___	___
6	5	4	1	3	2	1

Game On

Use the first word above to score bonus points in the Jungle Jump game in *Ready Set…Go Alef Bet!* online.

הַבְדָּלָה

| Hay | ה | WHAT'S NEW? |

Color the ה.

Complete the outline of the letter ה. Be sure it has a **H**ole in it. Then color the ה.

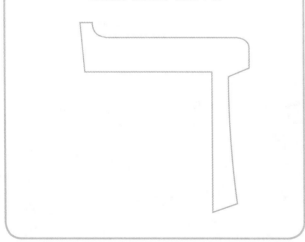

Letter Hint

The new letter ה looks like it has a **H**ole in it.

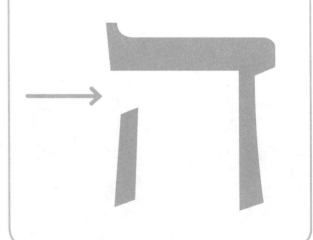

Now I Know My Alef-Bet!

Complete the **Hay**. Then write three on your own.

Take a Closer Look!

On each line circle all the letters that are the same as the one in the box.

ט	מ	ט	ט	מ	ט .1
כ	ב	כ	ב	כ	כ .2
י	ד	י	ד	ד	ד .3
ה	ת	ה	ה	ת	ה .4
ב	ת	ת	ב	ת	ת .5

46

I Can Understand Hebrew!

Your teacher will read these words to you:

the – הַ

יַלְדָה   יֶלֶד

 You're an Artist!

Your teacher will read these sentences to you.
Choose one sentence and draw it in the picture frame.

1. הַמּוֹרָה בַּכִּתָּה.

2. אָדָם יֶלֶד.

3. הַיֶּלֶד בַּכִּתָּה.

4. גִּילָה יַלְדָה.

5. הַיַּלְדָה בַּכִּתָּה.

6. דֶּגֶל בַּכִּתָּה.

7. הָעִפָּרוֹן עַל הַשֻּׁלְחָן.

Word Building

Read each line aloud.

START

קוּ	כֻּ	קְ	קוּ	כָּ	.1
הָא	הַ	הָא	הַ	הָ	.2
שׁוּ	שֶׁ	שַׁ	שֶׁ	שׁוּ	.3
מֵת	מָט	מֵת	מֵת	מַט	.4
בֵּם	בָּת	בָּם	בֵּם	בָם	.5

Game On

On each line above, circle any syllables that make a different sound from the others on the line. *Hint:* In some lines all of the syllables sound the same!

Write the circled syllables together to make a word you know. Start on the right.

_____

Circle the picture that matches your answer.

Use this word to score bonus points in the Hip Hop Hebrew game in *Ready Set…Go Alef Bet!* online.

48

tSUPER TZADEE （11）

 מִיץ　　　 צְדָקָה

| Final **TZ**adi ץ | **TZ**adi צ | **WHAT'S NEW?** |

 Word Building

Read each line aloud.

START

צוּ	צוֹ	צָ	צַ	צָ .1
קָ	קוֹ	כָ	קָ	כַ .2
שׁוֹם	שָׁם	גַם	אוֹם	אָ .3
דוֹם	דָ	דָם	צוֹם	צַ .4
קוּץ	גָץ	קָץ	בּוּץ	בַּ .5
מוּץ	כּוּץ	מַץ	גוּץ	אַץ .6

49

Letter Hint

The Y geTS up.

Letter Hint

The new letter Y geTS down on the floor.

Color the Y and Y.

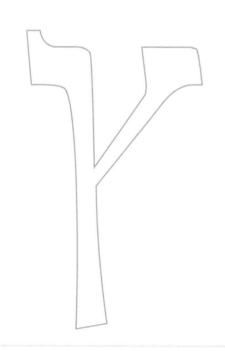

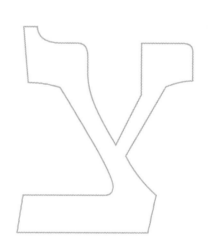

Now I Know My Alef-Bet!

Complete the **TZ**adi. Then write three on your own.

Complete the Final **TZ**adi. Then write three on your own.

I Can Understand Hebrew!

Your teacher will read these words to you.
Connect each word to the picture it describes.

כִּפָּה מְזוּזָה יָד הַבְדָלָה גֶּשֶׁם

קָדוֹשׁ דֶּגֶל בַּיִת מִיץ

בּוֹרֵא פְּרִי הַגָּפֶן

End Game

What sound do you hear at the end of each word? Your teacher will say each Hebrew word out loud. Circle the letter that ends each word.

צ	ד	ת	בּ	שׁ	
שׁ	צ	ג	ט	ם	
ק	ת	ג	ד	י	
ם	י	שׁ	כ	ד	
ד	ט	ק	צ	שׁ	
ג	ת	כ	ד	בּ	

Game On

What Hebrew letter did you circle twice? _____

Use this letter to score bonus points in the Zero Gravity game in *Ready Set…Go Alef Bet!* online.

VAVOOM! 12

כֶּלֶב

וָו

| Vet ב | Vav ו | WHAT'S NEW? |

Color the ו.

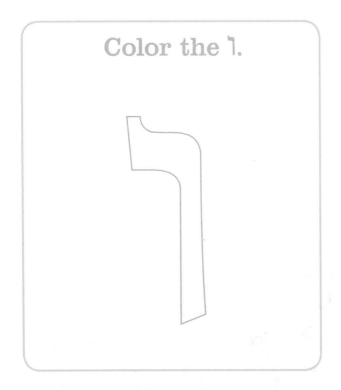

Letter Hint

The new letter ו looks like a person **V**aulting with a pole.

53

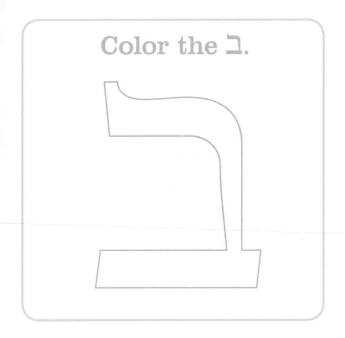

Color the ב.

Letter Hint

The new letter ב looks like a **Vacant Vat** because it is empty.

Now I Know My Alef-Bet!

Complete the **Vav.** Then write three on your own.

ו ‏וֹ ‏ו

Complete the **Vet.** Then write three on your own.

ב ‏בֿ ‏ב

Match Game

Match the letters and vowels that sound the same.

ם ‏בּוֹ ‏עֲ ‏ט ‏צ ‏ב ‏כ

ת ‏ץ ‏ק ‏ו ‏בְּ ‏מ ‏אָ

I Can Understand Hebrew!

Your teacher will read this word to you:

of, belonging to   שֶׁל

Your teacher will read these phrases to you. Match each phrase to its picture.

1. הַדָּג שֶׁל הַיֶּלֶד

2. הַדֶּגֶל בַּיָּד שֶׁל אִמָּא

3. הַכֶּלֶב שֶׁל הַיֶּלֶד

4. הָעִפָּרוֹן שֶׁל הַמּוֹרָה

5. הַדֶּגֶל בַּיָּד שֶׁל אַבָּא

6. הָעִפָּרוֹן שֶׁל הַיַּלְדָּה

Sound Check

The names of these objects sound similar in Hebrew and English. Circle all the objects that begin with the sound of the new letter וֹ.

Game On

Circle the name of the Hebrew letter that begins each word that is circled above.

דָב וָו בַּב

Use this letter to score bonus points in the Wacky Wheelbarrow game in *Ready Set…Go Alef Bet!* online.

לוּלָב

| Lamed | ל | WHAT'S NEW? |

Color the ל

to make it look like **L**ightning.

Letter Hint

The new letter ל looks like **L**ightning.

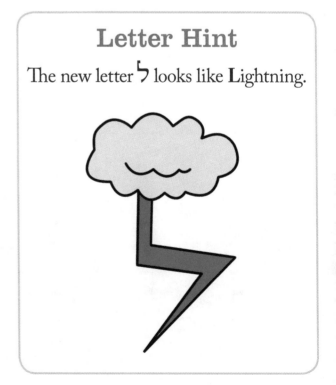

Now I Know My Alef-Bet!

Complete the Lamed. Then write three on your own.

Take a Closer Look!

On each line cross out all the letters that are different from the one in the box.

צ	ע	צ	צ	ע	צ .1
כ	ב	כ	כ	ב	כ .2
י	ו	ד	ו	י	י .3
ב	ה	ב	ת	ב	ב .4
ה	ת	ב	ב	ת	ת .5
ד	ו	ו	ו	י	ו .6

"String the Bead!"

"EE" = $\,$י $\Box$ $\Box$
 $\cdot$ $\cdot$

The new Hebrew vowel
looks like a little **bead**.
Color the bead.

 Word Building

Read each line aloud.

START

טִי	עֵ	מְ	שִׁי	תָּ	.1
הִי	בִי	לִי	כִּי	דְ	.2
הַ	וּ	לְ	דְּ	דַ	.3
הְת	עָם	גְל	קוּשׁ	דָם	.4
הִצְּיל אָבִיב גָלִיל		קָדוּשׁ	דָמִים		.5

59

I Can Understand Hebrew!

Your teacher will read this word part to you:

and   וְ–

Your teacher will read these phrases to you.
Check the phrase that matches each picture.

.1

☐ הַבַּיִת שֶׁל אַבָּא וְאִמָּא.

☐ הַבַּיִת בַּגֶּשֶׁם.

.2

☐ הַכֶּלֶב וְהַדָּג שֶׁל הַיֶּלֶד.

☐ הַכֶּלֶב בַּמַּיִם.

.3

☐ הַיֶּלֶד וְהַיַּלְדָּה בַּכִּתָּה.

☐ הַיֶּלֶד וְהַיַּלְדָּה בַּבַּיִת.

.4

☐ הָעִפָּרוֹן עַל שֻׁלְחָן.

☐ הַטַּלִּית וְהַתּוֹרָה עַל שֻׁלְחָן.

Beginning, Middle, or End?

Where do you hear the sound of the new letter ל? Your teacher will say the Hebrew name of each word out loud. Check ✓ all the places that you can hear the new sound. *Hint:* You may hear the sound twice in some words!

End	Middle	Beginning	

Game On

How many times did you hear the new letter in the middle of the word? _____

Use this number to score bonus points in the Jungle Jump game in *Ready Set…Go Alef Bet!* online.

שִׂמְחַת תּוֹרָה

סֻכּוֹת

Sin

Samech

WHAT'S NEW?

Color the ס.

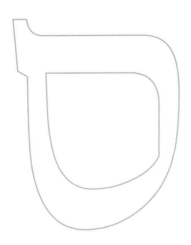

Letter Hint

The new letter ס looks like a **C**ircle.

Color the שׂ.

Letter Hint

The new letter שׂ looks like a Seal.

Now I Know My Alef-Bet!

Complete the **S**amech. Then write three on your own.

Complete the **S**in. Then write three on your own.

I Can Understand Hebrew!

Your teacher will read this word to you:

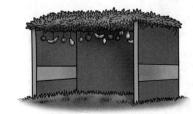

סֻכָּה

 Word Building

Read each line aloud.

שָׁ	לָ	קָ	כֶּ	אֶ	.1
שׁוּ	לוּ	כֶּ	קוּ	עֻ	.2
סִ	לִי	קָ	כִּ	עִ	.3
שִׂים	שָׁמִים	לוּלָב	קוּם	אָבִיב	.4

 You're an Artist!

Your teacher will read these sentences to you.
Draw in what is missing from the picture.

1. אַבָּא בַּסֻכָּה.

2. אִמָּא בַּסֻכָּה.

3. הַיֶּלֶד וְהַיַּלְדָּה בַּסֻכָּה.

4. הַסֻכָּה בַּגֶּשֶׁם.

5. הַכֶּלֶב בַּסֻכָּה.

6. הַלוּלָב שֶׁל אַבָּא בַּסֻכָּה.

Crack the Code

I'm like a "house" for a holiday,
But not for any vacation stay.
Crack the code and you will see
What my Hebrew name might be.

One of the objects on each line starts with a different sound from the others.
Circle the odd one out. Write the Hebrew letter it starts with in the box.

Copy the letters you wrote in the numbered spaces below.

_____   _____   _____
   3   2   1

Game On

Use the word above to score bonus points in the Hip Hop Hebrew
game in *Ready Set...Go Alef Bet!* online.

עִפָּרוֹן

נֵר

Final Nun ן   Nun נ   **WHAT'S NEW?**

Color the נ and the final ן.

Letter Hint

The new letter נ looks a Nose.
The ן looks like it's Nailed down.

Now I Know My Alef-Bet!

Complete the **N**un. Then write three on your own.

Complete the Final **N**un. Then write three on your own.

Sound Check

Circle all the items that begin with the sound of "נ."

Hint: You can look back to the Key Words on pages 26 and 66. All the other words are similar in Hebrew and English.

I Can Understand Hebrew!

Your teacher will read these words to you.
On each line, connect the words to their matching pictures.
Hint: Not every picture has a word.

וָו   צְדָקָה   עִפָּרוֹן   נֵר

לוּלָב   מְזוּזָה   סֻכָּה   כֶּלֶב

טַלִּית   שִׂמְחַת תּוֹרָה   תּוֹרָה   דֶּגֶל

Sound Advice

What sound do you hear in the middle of the word?
Circle the letter that is in the middle of each word.

ב	ל	ק	ג	ט	
ג	ט	כ	ל	ד	
ל	שׁ	ט	ד	ק	
ב	ג	ל	ד	כ	
כ	ב	ל	ס	ט	

Game On

Which letter is circled twice? _____

Use this letter to score bonus points in the Zero Gravity game in *Ready Set...
Go Alef Bet!* online.

מֶלֶךְ   בְּרָכָה   חַלָה

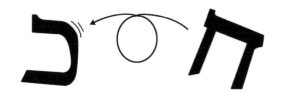

| Final Chaf ךּ | Chaf כ | Chet ח | **WHAT'S NEW?** |

Color the new Hebrew letters.

Letter Hint

The new letters ח and כ look similar when turned on their sides.

Now I Know My Alef-Bet!

Complete the **Ch**et. Then write three on your own.

חַ ‏ ‏ ‏ ‏ חַ

Complete the **Ch**af. Then write three on your own.

כּ ‏ ‏ ‏ ‏ כ

Complete the Final **Ch**af. Then write three on your own.

ךְ ‏ ‏ ‏ ‏ ך

Word Building

Read each line aloud.

נָ	כַ	שַׁ	חַ	לְ	סָ	.1
נוּ	חִ	סִ	כוּ	טִי	צוּ	.2
הִ	חִ	מִי	כִּי	לִי	צִ	.3
דָם	חַם	שָׁם	עַם	גַם	שָׁם	.4
דָן	כָּן	מָן	עָן	גַן	תַּן	.5

71

Sound Check

The names of these objects sound similar in Hebrew and English.
Circle all the objects that begin with the new letter ח.

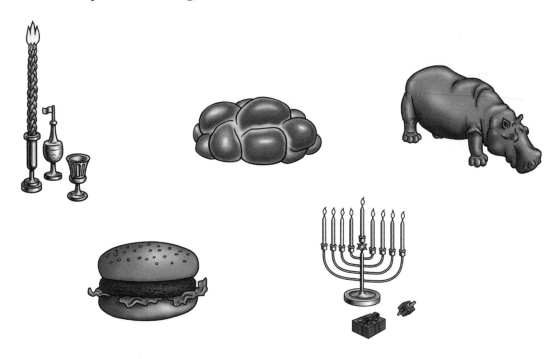

Sounds Right

Read each Hebrew syllable out loud.
Cross out the syllable on each line that sounds different.

4. שֹׁח סוּק סוֹק סוֹף   1. אַף אַק אָח

5. בִּיף בָּח בִּיךְ   2. נָח נִיךְ נִיק

3. רוּךְ רֶק רֶח

I Can Understand Hebrew!

Your teacher will read this word to you:

חָתוּל

Your teacher will read these sentences to you.
Check ✓ each sentence that describes the picture in the box.

.1

☐ הַמּוֹרָה בַּכִּתָּה.
☐ הַיַּלְדָּה אוֹכֶלֶת גְּלִידָה.
☐ הַיֶּלֶד וְהַיַּלְדָּה בַּכִּתָּה.

.2

☐ שַׁבָּת בַּבַּיִת.
☐ אַבָּא, אִמָּא וְהַיַּלְדָּה בַּבַּיִת.
☐ חַלָּה וְנֵר עַל הַשֻּׁלְחָן.

.3

☐ הַיֶּלֶד וְהַיַּלְדָּה בַּסֻּכָּה.
☐ הַיֶּלֶד וְהַכֶּלֶב בַּסֻּכָּה.
☐ הַלּוּלָב בַּיָּד שֶׁל הַיֶּלֶד.

.4

☐ הֶחָתוּל וְהַכֶּלֶב בַּכִּתָּה.
☐ הֶחָתוּל וְהַכֶּלֶב בַּסֻּכָּה.
☐ הֶחָתוּל וְהַכֶּלֶב בַּבַּיִת.

Make the Connection

Shabbat ends when we can see three of these on Saturday evening. Draw a straight line to connect the letters that make the same sounds.
Hint: Some of the letters are in English.

What do we look for at the end of Shabbat? Three _____

K

ס   שׁ

ק   כּ

S

N

ם   מ

נ   ז

M

ט

כ   ח

ת   תּ

ר

Which Hebrew letter above has the sound of **ch** and comes only at the end of a word? _____

Use this answer to score bonus points in the Wacky Wheelbarrow game in *Ready Set…Go Alef Bet!* online.

פֶּסַח

פּוּרִים

Pay

פ

WHAT'S NEW?

Color the פ.

Color פ Peppermint Pink!

Letter Hint

The new letter פ looks like it is Popping a Pink Peppermint.

Now I Know My Alef-Bet!

Complete the **P**ay. Then write three on your own.

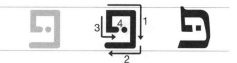

Sound Check

Cross out all the items that do not begin with the sound of "פ."

Hint: You can look back to the Key Words on pages 17 and 75. All the other words are similar in Hebrew and English.

"Oh, Oh—It's Over!"

"Oh" = וֹ ֹ

The new Hebrew vowel looks like a ball going over a letter. When you see a vowel **O**ver a letter, remember to say "**Oh!**"

 Word Building

Read each line aloud.

נוֹ	גוֹ	בֹ	לוֹ	פּוֹ .1
יוֹ	קוֹ	טֹ	אוֹ	בּוֹ .2
כִי	חָ	שַׁ	נַ	פָּ .3
דוֹב	גֵּב	צַו	סוֹב	אָב .4
סוֹף	בָּךְ	צַח	לָךְ	פַּח .5

I Can Understand Hebrew!

Your teacher will read these words and sentences to you:

אוֹכֵל   אוֹכֶלֶת   סָלָט

Connect the right food to each person.

3. אִמָא אוֹכֶלֶת סָלָט.   1. הַיֶלֶד אוֹכֵל פִּיצָה.

4. אַבָּא אוֹכֵל חַלָה.   2. הַיַלְדָה אוֹכֶלֶת גְלִידָה.

Beginning, Middle, or End?

Where do you hear the sound of the letters ח , כ, or ך? Your teacher will say the Hebrew name of each word out loud. Check all the places that you can hear the new sound.

End	Middle	Beginning	

Game On

How many times did you hear "ch" at the *end* of the word? _____

Use this number to score bonus points in the Jungle Jump game in *Ready Set…Go Alef Bet!* online.

רֶגֶל

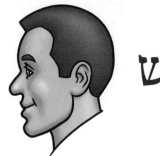

רֹאשׁ

Resh ר

WHAT'S NEW?

Color the ר.

Use the ר to draw a picture of your head.

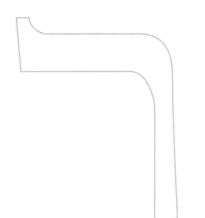

Letter Hint

The new letter ר is round. It looks like the **R**ound back of your head.

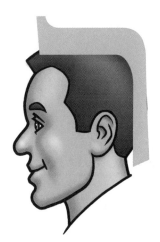

Word Building

Read each line aloud.

נֹ	גוֹ	לוֹ	ס	פּ	רוֹ	.1
מֹ	חוֹ	כֹ	שׁוֹ	בּוֹ	תֹ	.2
מוֹר	כֹר	קֹר	שׁוֹר	בּוֹר	טוֹר	.3
מֶר	חוֹר	כּוּר	צוּר	בָּר	תּוּר	.4
חֲמוֹר	חִבּוּר	כִּנוֹר	צִפּוֹר	בָּחוּר	מָרוֹר	.5

Now I Know My Alef-Bet!

Complete the **R**esh. Then write three on your own.

ר   ר   ר

Take a Closer Look!

On each line circle the letter that is the same as the one in the box.

תּ	כ	פּ	ט	בּ	**פּ** .1
ו	י	ג	נ	ר	**י** .2
ע	ט	מ	צ	ע	**צ** .3
ת	כ	ח	ת	ה	**ה** .4
צ	ע	ט	מ	צ	**ע** .5
שׁ	ע	שׁ	שׁ	שׁ	**שׁ** .6
ת	ח	ה	ת	כ	**ח** .7
ן	ו	י	ג	ץ	**ן** .8

Write your letter answers in the numbered spaces below.

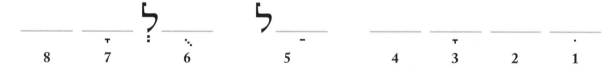

___ ___ לְ ___ לָ ___ ___ ___ ___
 8   7 6   5   4 3 2 1

Draw a picture of the words you wrote.

I Can Read Hebrew!

You can already read some real Hebrew words! Read them out loud.

4. שָׁלוֹם   3. שַׁבָּת   2. עִפָּרוֹן   1. עַל

8. מִיץ   7. קָדוֹשׁ   6. טַלִּית   5. רֹאשׁ

12. לוּלָב   11. סֻכּוֹת   10. יָד   9. פּוּרִים

I Can Understand Hebrew!

Read the words above again.
Then write the number of the word to the right of its picture.

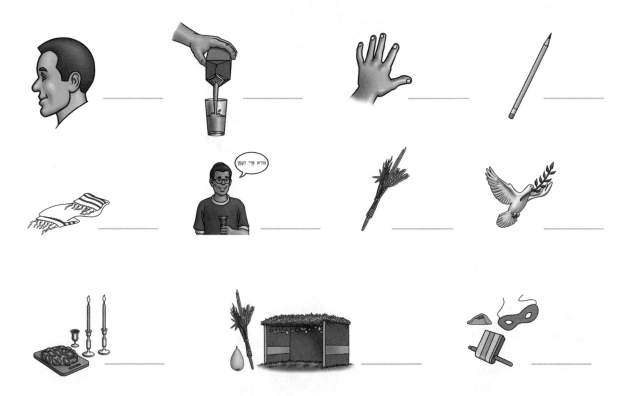

One word does not have a picture. Write it here: _____

Sound Check

Circle all the objects that begin with the new letter ר.
Hint: You can look back to the Key Words on pages 57 and 80. All the other words are similar in Hebrew and English.

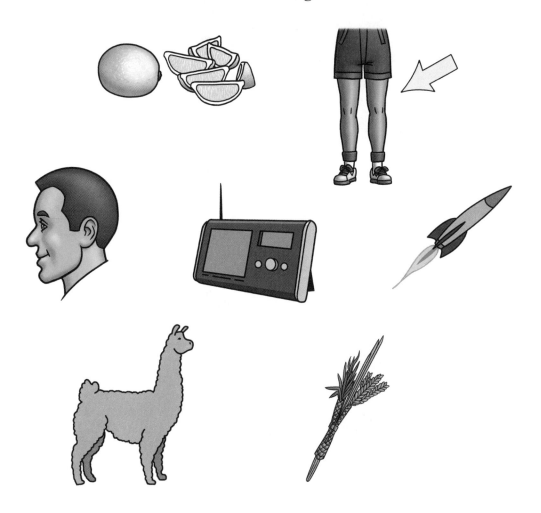

Game On

How many objects did you circle? _____

Use this number to score bonus points in the Hip Hop Hebrew game in *Ready Set…Go Alef Bet!* online.

זֶבְּרָה

Zayin ז WHAT'S NEW?

Color the ז.

Color the ז. Use different colors to make it **Zig-Zag**!

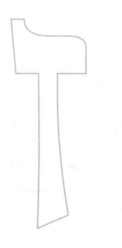

Letter Hint

The new letter ז looks like it makes a **Zig-Zag**.

Now I Know My Alef-Bet!

Complete the **Z**ayin. Then write three on your own.

Hidden Picture

Color in the hidden picture.

Green = "G"
Blue = "CH"
White = "Z"
Black = all other sounds

"Egg-xactly!"

"Eh" = ⬜ ⬜
⟋⟋ ⟋

The new Hebrew vowels
look like eggs in a nest.
When you see three dots
or five dots under a letter,
remember to say "Eh"!

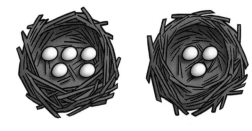

 Word Building

Read each line aloud.

זֶ	פֶּ	נֶ	כֶ	רֶ	עֶ .1
קַב	פֶּן	שֵׁם	חָו	לֶב	הֶב .2
רוּץ	פּוּז	זוּז	חוּץ	לוּז	עֹז .3
אֶלִי	פְּלִי	נֶלִי	חֶלוּ	רֶלוּ	הָלוּ .4
מֶשֶׁק פֶּרֶק		נָשָׁק	גְזוּז	רֶמֶז	אֱגוֹז .5

87

I Can Read Hebrew!

Here are some more real Hebrew words that you can read!
Read them out loud.

4. לוּלָב   3. כֶּלֶב   2. וָו   1. פֶּסַח

8. דֶּגֶל   7. מֶלֶךְ   6. רֶגֶל   5. דָג

11. חָתוּל   10. יֶלֶד   9. גֶשֶׁם

I Can Understand Hebrew!

Read the words above again.
Then write the number of the word to the right of its picture.

 _____ _____  _____ _____

 _____  _____  _____

 _____ _____ _____  _____

End Game

What sound do you hear at the end of each word? Your teacher will say each Hebrew word out loud.
Circle the letter that ends each word.

ל	בּ	כּ	ד	ב	
ר	ל	פּ	ן	ם	
ג	ם	ר	ק	נ	
פּ	ן	ל	ר	ם	
כּ	ב	בּ	ל	ד	
ז	ץ	ת	ד	ב	
ת	ץ	ז	בּ	כּ	

Game On

What Hebrew letter did you circle twice? _____

Use this letter to score bonus points in the Zero Gravity game in *Ready Set... Go Alef Bet!* online.

 אָלֶף   שׁוֹפָר

Final **Fay** ך **Fay** פ WHAT'S NEW?

Color the פ and ך.

Letter Hint

The new letter פ looks like a person's Face. The ך looks like a Flag.

90

Now I Know My Alef-Bet!

Complete the **Fay**. Then write three on your own.

Complete the Final **Fay**. Then write three on your own.

Match Game

Match the letters that sound the same.

מ   פ   ך   ס   נ   צ

ף   כ   ם   ץ   שׁ   ן

Take a Closer Look!

Circle the "twin letters" in each row.
Then write the circled letters in the spaces at the right.

צ	שׁ	שׂ	ע	שׁ	שׂ	שׂ	י	ו	ז	_____ .1
ן	י	ו	ז	ג	נ	ו	ר			_____ .2
ד	ץ	ף	ף	דּ	ף	ז	ק	פּ		_____ .3
ת	ח	ב	פּ	ט	פ	פּ	כ			_____ .4
ח	ה	ם	ס	ת	ח	ע	צ			_____ .5
נ	ר	ן	ז	דּ	ד	ר				_____ .6

Write your letter answers in the numbered spaces below.

.

_____ _____ _____ _____
  6   4   2   1

Circle the picture that the word describes.

I Can Read Hebrew!

Some of the Hebrew words below end in the sound "ah."
What letter ends those words?
Read these Hebrew words out loud to find the answer!

1. כִּפָּה   2. סֻכָּה   3. מוֹרָה   4. אוֹכֶלֶת

5. שׁוֹפָר   6. תּוֹרָה   7. אָלֶף   8. כִּתָּה

9. סָלָט   10. חַלָה

I Can Understand Hebrew!

Read the words above again. Then write the number of the word next to its picture. *Hint:* Two words describe one picture!

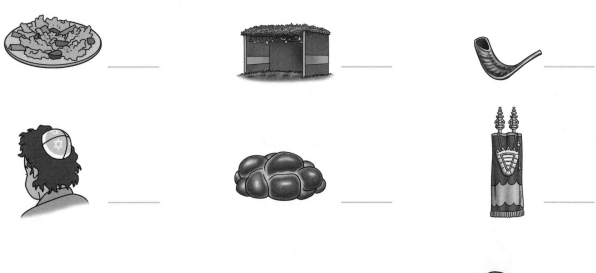

Crack the Code

Use the Picture Dictionary on pages 95 and 96 to find each of the Hebrew words pictured. Then write each word below its picture.

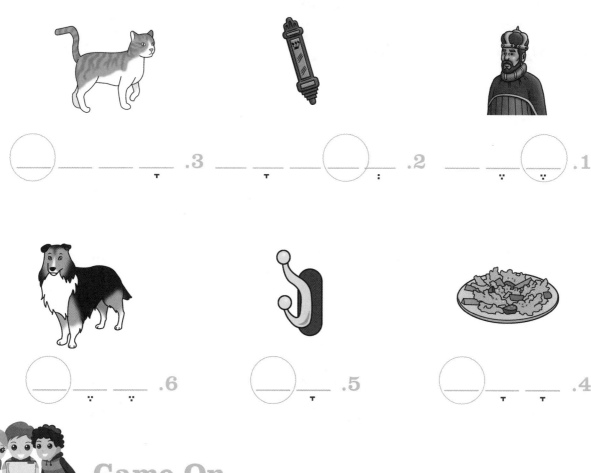

Game On

Write the letters you circled above to find a Hebrew phrase you can use to congratulate a classmate on how much Hebrew you have learned.

! ‗‗‗ ‗‗‗ ‗‗‗ ‗‗‗ ‗‗‗ ‗‗‗
   6   5   4   3   2   1

Use these words to score bonus points in the Wacky Wheelbarrow game in *Ready Set…Go Alef Bet!* online.

Pictionary

א

אַבָּא

אוֹכֵל

אוֹכֶלֶת

אָלֶף

אִמָּא

ב

בְּ־

בַּיִת

בְּרָכָה

ג

גְּלִידָה

גֶּשֶׁם

ד

דָּג

דֶּגֶל

ה

הַ־   the

הַבְדָּלָה

ו

וְ־   and

וָו

ז

זֶבְּרָה

ח

חַלָּה

חָתוּל

ט

טַלִּית

י

יָד

יָד

יֶלֶד

יַלְדָּה

כ

כֶּלֶב

כִּפָּה

כִּתָּה

95

ל	פ

לוּלָב

פּוּרִים

פֶּסַח

מ	צ

מוֹרָה

מְזוּזָה

מַיִם

מִיץ

מֶלֶךְ

צְדָקָה

נ	ק

נֵר

קִדוּשׁ

ס	ר

סֻכָּה

סֻכּוֹת

סָלָט

רֹאשׁ

רֶגֶל

ע	שׁ / שׂ

עַל

עִפָּרוֹן

שַׁבָּת

שָׁלוֹם

שׁוֹפָר

שֶׁל — of, belonging to

שִׂמְחַת תּוֹרָה

ת

תּוֹרָה